'Preciate Cha!

First Edition
20 19 18 17 16   5 4 3 2 1

Published by
Gibbs Smith
P.O. Box 667
Layton, Utah 84041

1.800.835.4993 orders
www.gibbs-smith.com

Designed by Sky Hatter
Printed and bound in Hong Kong
Gibbs Smith books are printed on either recycled, 100% post-consumer waste, FSC-certified
papers or on paper produced from sustainable PEFC-certified forest/controlled wood source.
Learn more at www.pefc.org.

Library of Congress Cataloging-in-Publication Data
Library of Congress Control Number: 2016930182
ISBN: 9781423644835

'Preciate Cha!

Illustrated by Sky Hatter

GIBBS SMITH
TO ENRICH AND INSPIRE HUMANKIND

YOU ARE A LIFESAVER!

'preciate cha!

What would
I ever do
without you?

PRESENT

You gave
me your time,

PAST

FUTURE

the most
thoughtful
gift of all.

—Dan Zadra

I can no other

answer make

but thanks,

And thanks; and

ever thanks.

—William Shakespeare

IT IS NOT HAPPY PEOPLE WHO ARE

THANKFUL,

BUT THANKFUL PEOPLE WHO ARE

HAPPY

Thank you for making me laugh, when I'd almost forgotten how.

—Pam Brown

WHEN LIFE IS SWEET, SAY THANK YOU AND CELEBRATE.

AND WHEN LIFE IS
BITTER, SAY
THANK YOU
AND
GROW.

If the only prayer
you say in your
life is thank you,
that would suffice.

—Meister Eckhart

I feel a very unusual sensation — if it is not indigestion, I think it must be GRATITUDE.

–Benjamin Disraeli

The smallest *act of kindness* is worth more than the *grandest intention.*

—Oscar Wilde

No DUTY is more urgent than that of returning THANKS.

—James Allen

I would thank you from the bottom of my heart, but for you my heart has no bottom

Take time
to be kind
&
to say
THANKYOU

-Zig Zigler

Thank you for your service.

We all have our down days, but it's not hard to smile and say, 'thank you.'

—Yvette Nicole Brown

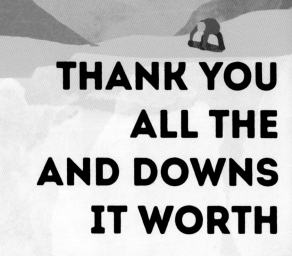

THANK YOU
ALL THE
AND DOWNS
IT WORTH

FOR LIFE AND LITTLE UPS THAT MAKE LIVING.

–TRAVIS BARKER

CÁM ƠN

ありがとう

Tha...

धन्यवाद

Ua tsaug rau

Děkuju

'Salama...

Gracia...

고맙습니다 Matur nuwu...

falemînderit

Dankie

Gràcies 謝謝

ευχαριστώ

kyou

شكرا

mèsi

Danke

Hvala

Merci

Dziękuję

Takk

Aitäh

Well, there's
not a day that
goes by

when I don't get up and say THANK YOU to somebody.

—Rod Stewart

BEFORE I GET OUT OF BED, I'M SAYING THANK YOU.
I KNOW HOW IMPORTANT IT IS TO BE THANKFUL.

—AL JARREAU

As we express our GRATITUDE, we must never forget that the highest APPRECIATION is not to utter words, but TO LIVE BY THEM.

—John F. Kennedy

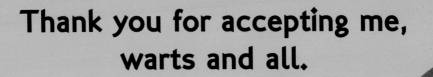

Thank you for accepting me,
warts and all.

Thank you for helping
me love myself.

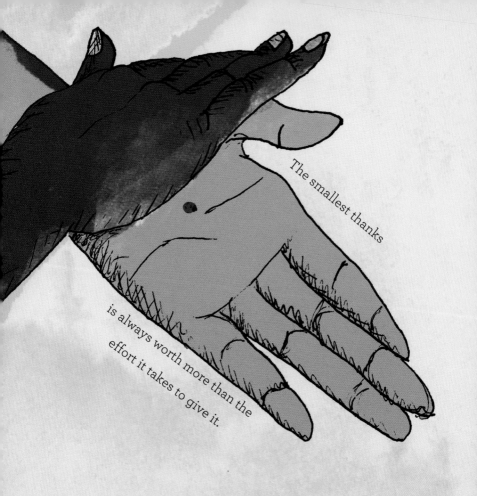

The smallest thanks is always worth more than the effort it takes to give it.

IF YOU CAN'T REWARD, THEN YOU SHOULD THANK.

— ARABIC PROVERB

EVERY TIME WE

REMEMBER TO SAY

THANK YOU,

WE EXPERIENCE NOTHING LESS THAN HEAVEN ON EARTH.

— SARAH BAN BREATHNACH

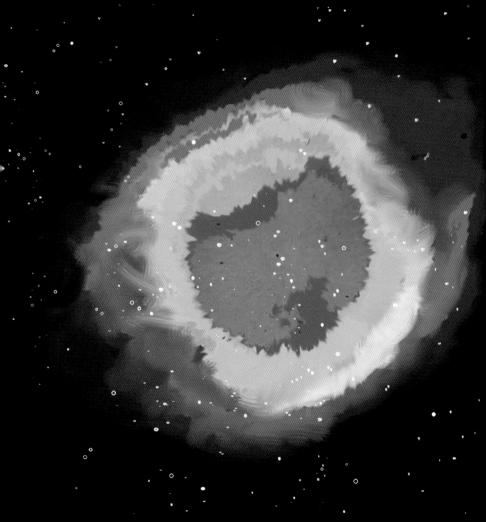

I would maintain that

THANKS

are the highest form of thought, and

that gratitude is happiness doubled by

WONDER.

– G.K. Chesterton

Thank you for letting me be cuckoo every once in a while.

Let us be grateful to people
who make us happy;

they are the charming
gardeners who make
our souls blossom.

– Marcel Proust

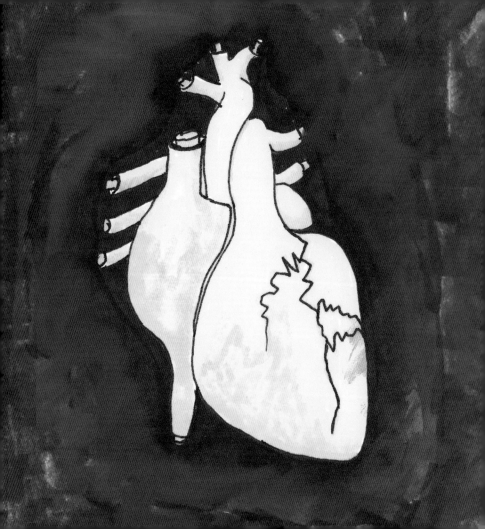

GRATITUDE

IS THE MEMORY OF THE

HEART.

– Jean Massieu

The only people with whom you should try to get even are those who have helped you.

— John E. Southard

BLESSED
are those who
can GIVE without
REMEMBERING and
RECEIVE
with out FORGETTING

—Elizabeth Bibesco

To say thank you, is in recognition of humanity.

—Toni Mont

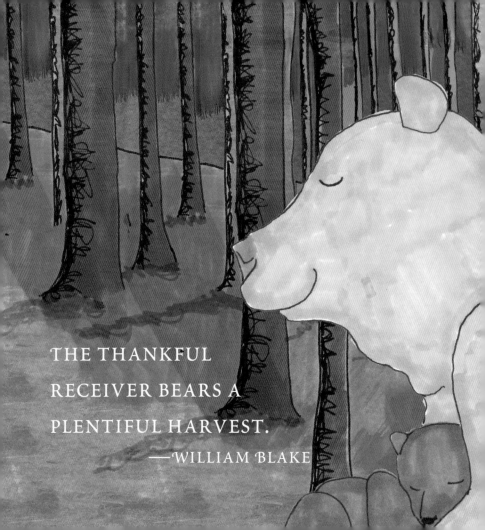

THE THANKFUL
RECEIVER BEARS A
PLENTIFUL HARVEST.
—WILLIAM BLAKE

Saying
thank you
is more than
good manners.

It is good
spirituality.

—Alfred Painter

#tha

nkful

Thank you for sharing your fries with me.

Thank you for

inspiring me.

UNIVERSE

FOR ALL THE GOOD THINGS IN MY LIFE

THAT I DON'T YET KNOW ABOUT

THANK YOU FOR BEING JUST AS WEIRD AS I AM.

O Lord, who lends me life;
lend me a heart replete
with thankfulness.

—William Shakespeare